Australia's Environmental Issues

FERAL ANIMALS

REDBACK publishing

Redback Publishing
PO Box 357 Frenchs Forest NSW 2086
Australia

www.redbackpublishing.com.au
orders@redbackpublishing.com.au

978-1-925860-27-6

Author: Peter Turner
Editor: Michael Anderson
Proofer: Marianne Lindsell
Designer: Redback Publishing

Originated by Redback Publishing

Reprinted 2022
Printed and bound in Malaysia

Acknowledgements
Abbreviations: l—left, r—right, b—bottom, t—top, c—centre, m—middle
We would like to thank the following for permission to reproduce photographs: (Images © shutterstock) p9t Nyangumarta Rangers - Department of Biodiversity, Conservation and Attractions, p15 Cane toad eggs - CSIRO

NATIONAL LIBRARY OF AUSTRALIA
A catalogue record for this book is available from the National Library of Australia

CONTENTS

Page 4 Introduction: Wild, Domestic and Feral
Page 6 How are Feral Animals Introduced?
Page 8 Endangering Australia's Native Animals
Page 10 Controlling Introduced Pets
Page 12 Cat - Scientific Name: Felis Catus
Page 14 Cane Toad - Scientific Name: Bufo Marinus
Page 16 Rabbit - Scientific Name: Oryctolagus Cuniculus
Page 18 Carp - Scientific Name: Cyprinus Carpio
Page 20 Red Fox - Scientific Name: Vulpes Vulpes
Page 22 Horse - Scientific Name: Equus Caballus
Page 24 Pig - Scientific Name: Sus Scrofa
Page 25 Water Buffalo - Scientific Name: Bubalus Bubalis
Page 26 Donkey - Scientific Name: Equus Asinus
Page 27 Goat - Scientific Name: Capra Hircus
Page 29 Getting It Right
Page 30 Find Out More
Page 31 Glossary
Page 32 Index

WILD, DOMESTIC AND FERAL

Introduced animals are animals brought to Australia by people, either deliberately or accidentally.

PROBLEM PESTS

Some feral animals that are now pests include:

- foxes
- cats
- cane toads
- pigs
- goats
- rabbits
- donkeys
- horses
- camels
- buffalo
- feral cattle
- some species of insects and birds

DOMESTIC VERSUS WILD

Domestic animals are those animals that live under the care of humans. Cattle, sheep and pet dogs and cats are all domestic animals. Wild animals live separately from humans. Kangaroos, magpies and tiger snakes are wild animals.

Sometimes, these definitions are not so clear. For example, the swallows that nest under roofs of houses and the spiders that scurry across ceilings are wild animals. They are simply using a house for shelter.

FERAL VERSUS WILD

Sometimes, domestic animals go wild. This means that they leave the care of humans and fend for themselves. These animals are feral animals. To 'go feral' means to 'go wild'.

In Australia, many species of introduced animals have become feral and are now serious pests. For example, rabbits cause hundreds of millions of dollars damage to Australian agriculture each year. They eat pasture so near to the ground that the soil is quickly eroded. Other introduced animals, such as the European goldfinch and the Bali banteng (a cow), are not regarded as serious pests.

WHY INTRODUCED SPECIES BECOME PESTS

There are several reasons why so many introduced species have been able to thrive in Australia:

Introduced animals may do well in Australia because there is a vacant niche, or place, for them. This is a space in the ecosystem that no native animal has taken up. For example, there are no large native grazing animals in Australia's far north, so water buffaloes were able to move in and thrive.

Many introduced animals, such as the cane toad, breed quickly, producing millions of eggs or many young.

The diseases that infect introduced species or the predators that eat them may not be found in Australia.

Changes to habitats caused by people have suited many introduced animals. Rabbits, for example, cannot live in Australia's forests. However, land that has been cleared for farming is suitable for rabbits, and they have thrived.

Different Names Same Problem

Introduced animals that become a problem are known as feral animals, predators or pests.

HOW ARE FERAL ANIMALS INTRODUCED?

Animals have been introduced into Australia both deliberately and accidentally.

Deliberately Introduced Species

Many species of animals have been brought to Australia and deliberately set free in the wild. Each time this happened, little thought was given to whether or not that animal might become a pest. Unfortunately, many introduced species did become pests. The ways animals were deliberately introduced include:

Acclimatisation Societies:
In the 1860s, acclimatisation societies aimed to introduce all sorts of animals (and plants) into Australia. They introduced birds such as sparrows, starlings and blackbirds as reminders of England. They also thought certain animals were better to look at or to hunt than Australian animals. For example, Sir Henry Barkly, a governor of Victoria in 1862, thought it would be a good idea to release monkeys into the bush to amuse bushwalkers.

Sport:
Foxes, rabbits, deer, hares and pheasants were introduced in the 1800s to provide hunters with prey. Hunters for recreation shot these animals.

Pest Control:
Cane toads, mosquito fish and Indian mynahs were released to control insect pests. These animals had no effect on the insect pests. Instead, they became pests themselves.

Accidentally Introduced Species

Many species of animals have accidentally arrived in Australia, and some of these have become pests. The ways in which animals have been, and are, accidentally introduced include:

When the ships of the First Fleet arrived in Sydney Cove in 1788, they accidentally carried many species of animals with them, including black rats and various types of insects. Some would have come abroad at Cape Town or Rio de Janeiro, ports the ships visited en route.

Animals may be carried in soil. For example, the Amazonian earthworm lives in some Queensland rainforests. Eggs of this animal probably arrived in a flowerpot from South America. The flowerpot snake from India managed to slip into Australia hidden in the soil of flowerpots.

Ballast is the water taken on board a ship when it has no cargo, to keep it stable at sea. When the ship is loaded at an Australian port, the ballast is dumped. More than 100 species of marine animals have arrived in Australia in ships' ballast. Some of these, such as the Northern Pacific seastar, have become serious pests.

Today, animals continue to be carried accidentally from country to country in ships and planes.

A Foxy Hoax?

Are there foxes in Tasmania? There have been sightings and many believe that foxes were set loose there by hunters around 2000. The Fox Eradication Program was set up. There was no evidence of fox activity collected since July 2011 so it was assumed that the fox eradication had been successful. Then in late 2016 a fox carcass was found. Some believe it was placed there as a hoax. There have been suggestions that earlier fox material, including fox poo, had also been planted in Tasmania. Opinion remains divided. One thing is known for sure; if foxes were to multiply in Tasmania, it would have a devastating impact on the native wildlife there.

ENDANGERING AUSTRALIA S NATIVE ANIMALS

Australia has the worst mammal extinction rate in the world. Globally, one out of three mammal extinctions in the last 400 years has occurred in Australia. Furthermore, over 1,700 plant and animal species are listed as threatened with extinction. Australia's desert mammals have suffered a very high extinction rate, with animals such as the lesser bilby and desert rat kangaroo gone forever.

While there are numerous reasons for this, a primary contributor to the loss of native species is feral animals. Introduced animals that have developed into pests cause havoc on native animal populations. Feral goats are a problem in Tasmania's rainforests. Feral pigs, cane toads and the Indian mynah have established populations in the Wet Tropics. Feral cats are ruthless predators that kill a staggering 20 billion native animals each year.

Predators and Australia's Endangered Species

The Department of the Environment and Heritage administers Australia's Endangered Species Protection Act. Recovery projects within organisations such as botanic gardens, zoos and universities are funded by the state and federal governments study and conserve threatened species.

There are a number of programs to tackle feral animals, and also provide native animals with ways to deal with predators.

- 50 metre long chicken wire tunnels are being placed around the Simpson Desert to allow small animals protection from predators. So far the results have been positive.
- Scientists are working with the Traditional Owners various communities and country to control cat and fox numbers.
- The government is currently testing new baiting methods for feral cats with the aim of culling up to 2 million of them. Animals rights groups oppose this as barbaric.

Feral animals impact native species in the following ways:

- They prey on native species.
- They compete for food and shelter.
- They destroy habitat.
- They spread diseases.

WHAT CAN YOU DO?

- Never dump a pet in the wild. They can survive and wreak havoc. Take unwanted pets to the RSPCA.

- If you have a cat, attach a bell to its collar. Make sure it does not catch native birds or other animals.

INDIGENOUS RANGERS

Aboriginal rangers are a vital part of protecting Australia's native species and the land from introduced predators. These rangers understand their country and undertake valuable environmental work across a diverse range of Australian habitats. Some of the significant work these rangers do is remove invasive animals and weeds, monitor biodiversity, revegetate and restore natural landscapes, deal with injured animals and use fire management to promote regrowth and biodiversity. Over 70 per cent of ranger groups work to protect threatened species across Australia.

CONTROLLING INTRODUCED PESTS

Hundreds of ships and planes enter Australia every week, each one could be carrying species that may become introduced pests. A lot of effort is made in Australia today to detect introduced pests before they do any damage.

At Airports

The Australian Quarantine and Inspection Service (AQIS) uses sniffer dogs at airports to find not only drugs, but plant and animal material. Passengers have been caught trying to smuggle in such things as live tortoises and snails.

SHIPPING TERMINALS

Many container ships arrive in Australian ports every day. These containers bring in all sorts of new species. AQIS officers inspect these containers for stowaways. For example, in 2005, a giant African snail was found on the underside of a container on a Malaysian ship docked in Fremantle. Also that year, Asian gypsy moth eggs were found on a foreign ship in Newcastle. This species is a serious pest of the timber industry overseas.

BY POST

Some people even send insects and animals to Australia by post. Australia Post lists all animals, alive and dead, including animal skins and hair products, as prohibited.

BIOLOGICAL CONTROL

Biological control is the use of natural enemies of an introduced pest species to control it. These enemies are called biological agents. When possible agents have been discovered in the pest's natural habitat, they are brought to Australia for testing. It is important that the agent attacks only the pest, so testing is essential before the agent can be released. Finding and testing biological control agents may take ten years or more.

Once released, a biological control agent may take several years to have an effect. Further, it may not completely eradicate a pest animal because when the pest's numbers fall, so too will the agent's. Many biological control agents die out in Australia before they can do their work. This may be due to the climate or even some Australian animals that attack the agent. Scientists may have to release several agents before the pest species is affected.

OTHER METHODS OF CONTROL

Controlling introduced pests can be hard, expensive work, especially if the pest species is allowed to get out of hand.

Conservation groups and farmers trap, shoot or poison introduced pests. These methods may remove many pests, but numbers soon build up again. Biological control of rabbits has been successful, but most other animal pests are not biologically controlled. Many people and groups, such as the Royal Society for the Prevention of Cruelty to Animals (RSPCA), are concerned about the inhumane killing of animal pests. For this reason, painless methods of control are being developed. Some of these control methods are viruses that make infected animals sterile, or unable to breed.

Complex Control Issues

In 1994, 16 dingoes were released on Townshead Island off the coast of Queensland to control 1,700 goats, but it took more than a decade to remove the dingoes after the goats were killed. More recently, in 2017 Hinchinbrook Shire Council was ordered to destroy two dingoes it had released on Pelorus Island to kill the feral goats there. The dingoes were fitted with suicide collars designed to release a deadly pill that would euthanize them once the goats had been eradicated, however the tracking systems in these collars weren't working. Instead of killing goats, the dingoes were killing rare birds and other animals. Animals rights groups oppose the dingo method of culling feral goats, saying it is cruel and that sniper shooting would be more effective and humane.

CAT – SCIENTIFIC NAME: FELIS CATUS

One of the most destructive animals to be introduced to Australia is the cat. Cats arrived with European settlement and are now considered to be the single biggest threat to Australia's native animals. Feral cats are different to domestic cats and stray cats in that they live and reproduce in the wild and survive by hunting or scavenging. They have no need for humans.

Since the British arrived in 1788, about 11 per cent of Australia's 273 native mammals have gone extinct, with a major factor being the introduction of cats. The threat of feral cats to Australia's native species is greater than of any other predator, and substantially more of a threat than the loss of habitat. Feral cats cover 99.8 per cent of Australia at a density of one cat for every four square kilometres.

Why Are They A Problem?

Feral cats are efficient hunters and it's estimated feral cats eat 75 million native animals a night—more than 20 billion mammals, reptiles, birds and even insects every year. They prey mainly on small native wildlife. On some islands, cats have caused the extinction of native bird, mammal and reptile species. However, not all of their hunting is harmful to native wildlife, as feral cats also prey on rabbits, another problem pest. Cats may carry toxoplasmosis, a disease that can kill native mammals. If the deadly disease rabies ever reaches Australia, feral cats would hasten its spread throughout the country.

The three main groups of cats in Australia:

1. pet cats, which are cared for by their owners;
2. stray cats, which roam city streets and may get hand-outs from people;
3. feral cats, which live apart from humans.

CATASTROPHIC!

A PAIR OF BREEDING FERAL CATS THAT HAVE TWO OR MORE LITTERS PER YEAR CAN EXPONENTIALLY PRODUCE 420,000 OFFSPRING OVER A SEVEN-YEAR PERIOD.

BACKGROUND BRIEF

Cats were first domesticated from African wildcats in Egypt 5,500 years ago. No one knows for certain when cats first arrived in Australia. There were some on the First Fleet in 1788, but cats may have already been in Australia, descended from animals washed ashore from shipwrecks more than 100 years earlier. In the late 1800s, cats were deliberately released into the wild to control rabbits. Australia's estimated 10 million feral cats are descendants of these animals and of domestic cats dumped by their owners. People still dump unwanted kittens in the cities and bushland.

WHAT IS BEING DONE ABOUT THEM?

On some islands, cats have been eradicated completely by trapping, baiting and shooting. On mainland Australia, control of feral cats is more difficult. The cats are elusive and avoid humans, and they usually hunt at night and hide in dens during the day, making them very difficult to find. If cats are moved from an area, others soon move in. In some places, cat-proof fences have been built to protect certain rare native species, such as bilbies. But these fences are expensive, which means only small areas can be kept cat-free. To reduce the numbers of unwanted cats, which may become stray or feral, cat owners are encouraged to de-sex their pets. About $6 million will be spent 'humanely' shooting, trapping and poisoning feral cats, with the aim of killing 2 million by 2020.

Solving One Problem After Another

Cats were taken by sealers to Macquarie Island, south of Tasmania, soon after it was discovered in 1810. By 1820, feral cats were preying on the sea birds that nest on the island. Soon, two Macquarie Island birds, the rail and the parakeet, became extinct and other bird species were endangered. A trapping, baiting and shooting program to eradicate the cats began in 1998, and by 2000 the Tasmanian Government declared the island to be cat free. Unfortunately rats and rabbits remained a problem, especially without the cats to keep their numbers down. From 2007, the focus was on eradicating these pests from the island. In 2014, Macquarie Island was officially declared pest free.

CANE TOAD – SCIENTIFIC NAME: BUFO MARINUS

The cane toad has become a greater problem than most other introduced animals.

Why Are They A Problem?

Cane toads will eat almost anything they can fit into their mouths. This includes lizards, frogs, insects and even other cane toads. The skin of a cane toad is poisonous, and many native animals and pet dogs have been killed within a few minutes of eating a toad. Cane toads can squirt venom at attackers from glands on their shoulders. Cane toad tadpoles and eggs are also poisonous.

BACKGROUND BRIEF

Cane toads originated in northern South America. In 1935, cane toads were released at Gordonvale in north Queensland. These toads were descendants of animals from Hawaii, where they had also been introduced. Cane toads were brought here to control the native greyback cane beetle, a pest of the sugar cane industry. However, the beetles spend most of their time in the leaves, where the toads are unable to reach them. By 1938, the cane toad had already spread too far for it to be stopped. By 2000, cane toads had reached the wetlands of Kakadu National Park in Northern Territory. By 2007, they had reached Darwin. They may soon spread to the Pilbara and Kimberly regions of Western Australia.

ABILITY TO BREED

A female cane toad can produce 30,000 eggs a month. The toxins on these eggs kill the eggs of native frogs. In three days, the cane toad eggs hatch into jet-black tadpoles. Cane toads need only small pools of water for breeding and can even survive in salty water.

WHAT IS BEING DONE ABOUT THEM?

The cane toad has poisonous skin, eggs and tadpoles, killing native animals and pets that eat these. However some native animals have adapted ways of avoiding the venom. Water rats, crows and kites turn the toads upside down and tear open the skin to eat the toad's insides.

As of 2017, environmentally friendly traps are being trialled in Queensland to stop the toads while in tadpole phase. The traps use adult cane toad poison to eradicate up to 10,000 juveniles at a time.

RABBIT – SCIENTIFIC NAME: ORYCTOLAGUS CUNICULUS

The European rabbit has probably caused the most damage of any introduced animal. When rabbits were at their most numerous, there may have been 800 million of them in Australia.

Why Are They A Problem?

Rabbits causes erosion by eating pastures and plants close to the ground. They compete with native mammals for food and may have caused extinction of many native plants. They cause about $600 million worth of damage to Australia's farm production each year and compete with cattle and sheep for grass. They eat pastures and graze plants so close to the ground that the soil is soon washed or blown away.

BACKGROUND BRIEF

The European rabbit comes from Spain. The first 24 wild rabbits were released in Australia in 1859 by a sheep farmer called Thomas Austin on his property near Geelong, Victoria. Austin wanted these animals to breed so that he had rabbits to hunt. Nine years later, he reported that 14,253 rabbits had been shot on his land. By 1910, rabbits had spread across Australia as far as they could go. They are now across mainland Australia, except in the tropical north.

Rabbit Proof Fence

Europeans brought rabbits to Australia for food and to be used for hunting. The rabbits quickly bred and spread and have caused considerable damage to the natural environment. In the early 1900s, a barbed wire fence was erected to keep rabbits out of Western Australia's farmlands. It stretched 3,256 kilometres from north to south across Western Australia. The original fence was followed by two more fences. The rabbit proof fence is the longest fence in the world. It is estimated that there are now 200 million rabbits in Australia, competing with native animals for food and shelter. They have contributed to the decline or loss of the southern and northern hairy-nosed wombats, the greater bilby, yellow-footed rock wallaby, the mallee fowl and the plains-wanderer.

WHAT IS BEING DONE ABOUT THEM?

Until 1950, there was no effective control for rabbits. Shooting, trapping, ferreting (where ferrets are put into a rabbit burrow to drive the rabbits out), poisoning and destruction of burrows could kill only a small percentage of rabbits. These methods also took a lot of effort. In 1950, the first biological control for rabbits was introduced. It was a virus from South America that causes myxomatosis, a disease spread by mosquitoes and fleas. It killed up to 90 per cent of Australia's rabbits, but this success was not followed up with other controls, and soon the rabbit population increased again from those that survived. Today, many rabbits have become resistant to the virus, and the virus itself has become less virulent (powerful).

In 1995, a new virus was introduced into Australia's rabbit population. Rabbit calicivirus disease, or RCD, has killed millions of rabbits since then. In some areas of central Australia, native mammals have increased in numbers and many plants have reappeared since RCD was released. There have been a number of variants on the original strain released since then.

CARP – SCIENTIFIC NAME: CYPRINUS CARPIO

Many people think of carp as "rabbits of the river". Today, in most of the Murray River, there are more carp than any other fish.

Why Are They A Problem?

Carp suck mud from the bottoms of river and lakes and strain invertebrates from it. This feeding behaviour makes the water murky and can prevent many aquatic plants from taking root, thereby damaging the habitat of native fish. Because of this, carp are blamed for the fall in numbers of native fish in the Murray River. However, scientists say that dams and weirs, fertilisers and grazing have also contributed to the river's problems. Dams and weirs have changed the river's flow, fertilisers have caused increased growth of algae, and grazing has damaged riverbank vegetation.

BACKGROUND BRIEF

Carp come from central Asia. Some were released into Sydney's Prospect Reservoir in 1907, but it was not until the 1960s that carp found their way into the Murray River. The carp in the Murray had been imported illegally from Germany, and were washed into the river during a flood. Since then, the carp have spread to most rivers and creeks of the Murray-Darling River Basin, Australia's largest catchment.

A Matter of Taste

Few people in Australia like eating carp. It has brown flesh and is very bony. However, carp are exported to countries where people do eat the fish. There is a company in Australia that catches carp and mashes them to make organic fertilser.

WHAT IS BEING DONE ABOUT THEM?

Carp have been removed from some wetlands along the Murray River by fishing or poisoning. Screens have been put up to prevent carp from re-entering these places. In the river itself, these methods would not be effective, and the best method of control may be to manage the river properly. Poor management practices have affected fish in the river, with numbers of native fish decreasing as numbers of carp increase. Seasonal floods, which help native fish disperse, are reduced by dams and weirs. When cattle are allowed to trample the river's edge, they destroy the habitat for native fish. In the same way, removing logs from the river for boat traffic reduces shelter and breeding places for native fish. With good management, the balance could tip back the other way, making the river more suitable for its native fish, and less so for carp.

As part of the Federal Government's $15 million commitment to reduce carp by 95 per cent by 2045, the National Carp Control Plan (NCCP) includes the possibility of releasing the virus cyprinid herpesvirus 3 (the carp virus) as a bio-control agent. The earliest release for the carp herpes virus is late 2018.

RED FOX – SCIENTIFIC NAME: VULPES VULPES

Foxes pose a serious problem in Australia, with current estimates around 6.2 million of this apex predator. Several species of native animals have become extinct on mainland Australia because of foxes. Some of these animals, such as the golden bandicoot, now survive only on offshore, fox-free islands.

Why Are They A Problem?

Australia's native wildlife has suffered enormously because of foxes. Animals such as eastern barred bandicoots in Victoria, bilbies in central Australia and numbats in Western Australia are easy prey for these predators. Foxes also prey on lambs and may kill more than 40 per cent of the lambs born on a single farm. Even native predators such as spot-tailed quolls are affected by foxes for prey. Foxes also spread seeds of weeds, such as blackberry, in their droppings.

BACKGROUND BRIEF

People who enjoyed fox-hunting released the first European red foxes in Australia near Melbourne in 1885. With each vixen able to breed at ten months of age and produce up to ten cubs a year, numbers quickly increased. By 1920, foxes had reached Western Australia. Foxes are now found across mainland Australia, except in the tropical north.

WHAT IS BEING DONE ABOUT THEM?

Shooting is one method of fox control, but on its own is not very effective. In 2007, Victoria ended a fox-control program in which a $10 bounty was paid for each foxtail. Under this program, 63,174 foxes were shot. The program was stopped because poison-baiting and destruction of dens are believed to be more effective ways of reducing fox numbers.

A CONUNDRUM

Foxes kill native wildlife, so they are pests too. Rabbits compete with native wildlife so they are pests too. But foxes kill rabbits, which must help native wildlife. Further native wildlife, such as eagles, eat rabbits. Clearly the interaction between foxes, rabbits and native wildlife is not simple. In planning to control foxes, the effects on rabbits and native wildlife must therefore be considered.

HORSE – SCIENTIFIC NAME: EQUUS CABALLUS

Feral horses, or brumbies, have become part of Australian folklore, almost as if they are native animals. The Man from Snowy River by 'Banjo' Paterson is one of Australia's most well-known poems. It romanticises the place of horses in the Australian bush. Australia has the largest wild horse population of anywhere in the world and these feral horses are serious pests. And yet, there is much debate about the role these animals now play in the country's culture and history.

Why Are They A Problem?

Horses can do a lot of damage to soil and plants. With their heavy bodies and hard hooves, they wear tracks in the soil, causing erosion. Because of their weight, horses can destroy the burrows of animals, such as the bilby, as they can walk over them. Horses compete with native animals for grass, and their presence at waterholes scares smaller animals. Feral horses have a major effect on the cattle industry because they compete with cattle for grass. Most of Australia's 400,000 feral horses live in the grazing country of Western Australia, the Northern Territory and Queensland. There are about 6,000 in Kosciuszko National Park.

BACKGROUND BRIEF

Horses have been domesticated for around 5,000 years. Their ancestors were wild horses of Asia, such as Przewalski's horses of Mongolia. Along with other hoofed animals, such as sheep and cattle, horses arrived in Australia with the First Fleet in 1788. By 1804, there were reports of wild horses in the new colony. These horses had escaped from farms. Later, when motorised transport and farm machinery were introduced, many workhorses were set free to join the wild herds. Today, brumbies are found across the Australian mainland, from the mountains of the southeast to the grasslands of central Australia and to the tropical far north.

WHAT IS BEING DONE ABOUT THEM?

Shooting horses from helicopters is expensive, but is also probably the best way to keep horse numbers down. Sometimes, feral horses are rounded up and sold as pets, or for pet food. Traps are sometimes set near waterholes. The traps have one-way gates that let animals in for a drink but stop them from leaving. Natural disasters, such as droughts, affect brumby numbers. The battle continues between those who support the culling of brumbies and those who oppose it.

PIG – SCIENTIFIC NAME: SUS SCROFA

Australia's feral pigs are descended from European breeds, which were domesticated thousands of years ago from wild pigs. In 1776, Captain James Cook released a boar (male pig) and a sow (female pig) in Tasmania. The animals did not survive. Pigs were also released on the mainland of Australia by other explorers, to provide food for settlers.

Today, there are millions of feral pigs in Australia. They prefer areas that have a reliable water supply. For this reason, there are no feral pigs in Australia's deserts. Most of Australia's 24 million feral pigs are found in New South Wales, Queensland and the north of the Northern Territory.

Why Are They A Problem?

Feral pigs eat pastures and crops such as rice and sugar cane, kill and eat lambs, and damage fences. Feral pigs root up native plants, and feed on ground-nesting birds and their eggs, including cassowary chicks and eggs. They also prey on frogs, lizards and small mammals. They turn waterholes into mud pools when they wallow in them during hot weather. Feral pigs also carry diseases that can be spread to cattle and sheep. In 2017, a disease called swine brucellosis arrived in New South Wales, carried by feral pigs from Queensland. It can be transmitted to humans.

WHAT IS BEING DONE ABOUT THEM?

Feral pigs breed quickly; a sow can produce 14 piglets a year. This means that even if the number of pigs is reduced to only a few, their population can quickly increase. Dingoes and saltwater crocodiles prey on pigs, and recreational shooters shoot many pigs. Trapping is the most effective method of controlling feral pigs. A pig trap is a wire enclosure that is baited with food. The pigs enter the trap, and their feeding eventually sets off a bar that causes the trap door to close. Poisoning is also used, but as there is no bait specific to pigs, domestic dogs and other animals can also be poisoned. Scientists hope one day to control feral pig numbers by reducing their fertility, so they produced fewer offspring.

WATER BUFFALO – SCIENTIFIC NAME: BUBALUS BUBALIS

There are two types of water buffalo in Australia; one from western Asia, with curled horns, and the other from eastern Asia, with swept-back horns. They are both descendants of the wild Asian buffalo, which is now endangered. About 80 water buffaloes were brought to Australia from Indonesia between 1825 and 1843. They were taken to settlements in the far north of the Northern Territory, but when the settlements were abandoned in 1849, so too were the buffaloes. By 1985, there were more than 340,000 feral water buffaloes living in the wetlands of the Top End of the Northern Territory. The water buffalo can grow to a weight of 1,200 kilograms.

Why Are They A Problem?

A large animal that lives in a herd can do a lot of environmental damage, especially in places where such large animals have not lived for thousands of years. Water buffaloes trample native plants, and wallow in wetlands, which keeps the animals cool in hot weather but also muddies the water. As the buffaloes move through the wetlands, they can create swim channels that provide ways for seawater to enter the wetlands. Seawater contains salt, which kills wetland plants, such as swamp paperbark forests, and freshwater animals. Water buffaloes also carry diseases that can spread to domestic stock. For example, brucellosis is a disease that causes cows to abort their developing claves.

WHAT IS BEING DONE ABOUT THEM?

Because of the threat they pose to the environment and to cattle, a mass shooting of water buffaloes was undertaken from 1979 to 1997. The animals were shot mainly from helicopters. This reduced water buffalo numbers drastically. Some people regret this because the water buffalo had become a symbol of the Northern Territory. Water buffaloes are also hunted for pet meat, for human consumption and by trophy hunters (people who are guided to a bull water buffalo to shoot it and pose next to it for a photograph). Today, water buffaloes are found mainly in Arnhem Land, in the Northern Territory. There is a small herd of a few hundred in Kakadu National Park. The Indigenous people there have been given permission by the government to keep this herd for meat.

Elsewhere in the world, buffalo provide meat and dairy for billions of people. In Australia, the buffalo is treated as a pest instead of a potential resource.

DONKEY – SCIENTIFIC NAME: EQUUS ASINUS

Donkeys have been used by people for more than 4,000 years, ever since the wild ass of northern Africa was first domesticated by the ancient Egyptians. Today, donkeys run wild in many parts of inland Australia. Donkeys were first brought to Australia in 1866, to be used as pack animals to carry supplies to remote areas in the outback. By the 1920s, people had reported seeing large wild herds, and in 1949 the donkeys was listed as serious pest in Western Australia. Today, there are millions of wild donkeys in Australia.

Why Are They A Problem?

On outback cattle stations, donkeys compete with cattle and sheep for grass. They also compete with native grazing animals, such as red kangaroos. When their numbers are high, donkeys may overgraze native plants. The ground loses its cover of vegetation and the soil is eroded by wind and water and more susceptible to erosion. Donkeys can go for longer without water and eat a wider range of plants than horses and cattle. This means they can survive in areas where horses and cattle cannot. As feral animals, it also means they can cause greater damage to native vegetation than these other animals.

WHAT IS BEING DONE ABOUT THEM?

Shooting from helicopters is probably the most effective, but also the most expensive, method of donkey control. In 2017, 6,000 feral animals were shot from helicopters in the Kakadu National Park under a feral animal eradication program, including thousands of donkeys.

GOAT – SCIENTIFIC NAME: CAPRA HIRCUS

Goats arrived in Australia in 1788 on board the First Fleet. These animals were ideal for settlers in a strange land because they ate a wide range of grasses and leaves, they were managed easily and they provided meat, milk and hair (such as mohair). When settlers moved inland, they took goats with them. The feral goat herds of Australia are descended from domestic goats that took off on their own or were dumped when their owners no longer had any use for them. There may be up to three million feral goats in Australia today, most of them living in the dry inland.

Why Are They A Problem?

Goats compete with native animals for food, water and shelter. Goats also cause erosion. Their hard hooves damage the fragile soil of inland Australia, which is then more easily blown or washed away. Goats carry diseases and parasites, such as footrot and tapeworms.

WHAT IS BEING DONE ABOUT THEM?

Dingoes prey on goats, and where there are dingoes goat numbers are low. However, dingoes also prey on sheep, and where dingoes are controlled, feral goat numbers may be high. Shooting goats from helicopters and trapping them at waterholes are often used as control methods. The 'Judas' method involves trapping a feral goat and releasing it with a radio-collar attached. The goat then leads shooters to the herd via the radio signal emitted from the collar.

CAMELS

Australia is the only country with wild one-humped camels, or dromedaries. In their original lands, camels are domesticated. Australia's wild camels descended from animals once used for transport in inland Australia. With the arrival of cars, many of these animals were set free and formed feral mobs. Camels are well suited to life in the desert.

YELLOW CRAZY ANT

The yellow crazy ant is considered to be one of the world's 100 worst invasive alien species. Yellow crazy ants outnumber and displace other species, and then dominate food and nesting resources. It is too late to eradicate them in Queensland.

The yellow crazy ant is also a major problem on Christmas Island. Christmas Island flying foxes are essential to the rainforest ecosystem because they disperse seeds and assist pollination. The flying fox are under threat because of loss of habitat due to yellow crazy ants, which swarm the tree canopies.

Christmas Island

Christmas Island is home to many unusual native species that are now at risk of extinction due to threats that include yellow crazy ants and other introduced predators such as cats and rats. Mammals such as the Maclear's rat and bulldog rat are now extinct. The Christmas Island shrew is generally believed to also be extinct now.

Lord Howe Island Rodent Eradication Project

Introduced rodents have wreaked havoc to a number of native species on Lord Howe Island, including the Lord Howe Island phasmid (stick insect) and the island's highly diverse snail fauna.

Lord Howe Island has 62 species of snail of which 59 are endemic to the island. One species is believed to be extinct, while five are currently listed as Endangered or Critically Endangered. There is now a program in place to eradicate the rodents from Lord Howe Island to protect the remaining snails, and other species at risk.

GETTING IT RIGHT

Not all introduced species have a harmful effect on the environment. There are a number of species that have been introduced and have a benign or even beneficial impact on the environment.

EARTHWORMS

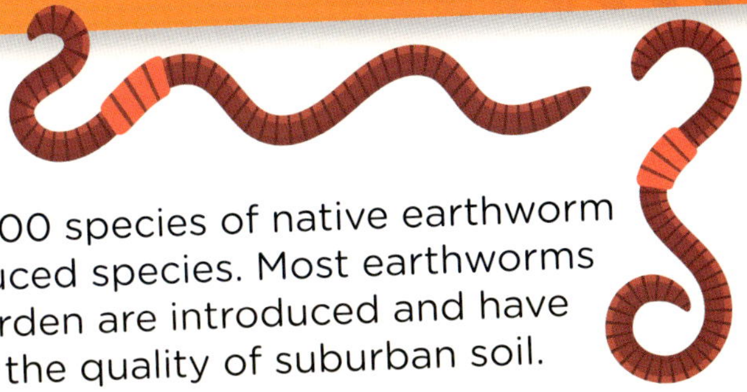

Australia has about 1,000 species of native earthworm and another 75 introduced species. Most earthworms you see around the garden are introduced and have contributed greatly to the quality of suburban soil.

DUNG BEETLE

The dung beetle was brought to Australia to deal with agricultural industry's cattle dung problem. The introduced beetles have been effective in dealing with this.

MONARCH BUTTERFLY

The Monarch Butterfly was introduced to Australia in 1871 to help control a weed called the milk bush plant, which was taking over large areas of New South Wales and Queensland. The monarch caterpillars only feed on milkweed, so the introduction of this species has helped to control it.

Now, due to loss of habitat and widespread use of pesticides, milkweed is disappearing and the monarch butterflies are at risk.

FIND OUT MORE

SEARCH KEY WORDS

Endangered, threatened species, vulnerable species, habitats, conservation, ecosystem, myxomatosis, baiting, feral animals, invasive species.

SOURCES

http://www.environment.gov.au
https://invasives.org.au
http://www.environment.gov.au/biodiversity/invasive-species/
http://www.iucnredlist.org

WATCH

http://www.abc.net.au/btn/story/s2421873.htm

Some organisations that provide more information:

Australian Wildlife Conservancy
http://www.australianwildlife.org

The Foundation for Australia's Most Endangered Species (FAME)
https://www.fame.org.au/projects

WWF Australia
http://www.wwf.org.au

GLOSSARY

amphibian - an animal with a backbone that develops in water but it spends its adult life on land, such as frogs and toads

aquatic - found in water

bounty - payment made for killing a pest animal

catchment - the area of land that drains into a river

climate - the average weather condition over a long period of time

drought - prolonged period of very little or no rainfall

ecosystem - a community of organisms that interact with one another and with the environment in which they live (e.g. a pond)

erosion - the process of wearing away of the land, usually by wind and water

extinction - the end of the existence of a species

habitat - the place where an animal or plant usually lives or grows

immune - unaffected by disease

immunocontraception - a form of biological control that aims to stop rabbits from breeding

invertebrate - an animal that does not have a backbone (e.g. worms, insects, snails)

mammal - a vertebrate animal (has a backbone) that drinks milk from its mother when young

marsupial - a mammal that is born undeveloped and completes its development in its mother's pouch

myxomatosis - a disease of rabbits caused by the myxoma virus

myxoma virus - a virus carried from rabbit to rabbit by fleas or mosquitoes

native - a plant or animal living in its country of origin

organic fertiliser - fertilizer made from plant or animal matter

parasite - an animal or plant that lives in or on another animal or plant (the host)

predator - an animal that kills and eats other animals

rabbit calicivirus disease (RCD) - a highly infectious disease of rabbits that causes death within 30 to 40 hours

rabies - a disease that affects mammals

stowaway - an animal that is unknowingly carried on ships and planes

toxin - poison

venom - poison produced by some animals and plants

virus - microscopic agents that infect animals and plants

weir - a barrier across a river or stream that is used to retain water and prevent it from going downriver

wetlands - places that are covered with water some or all of the time

INDEX

A
acclimatisation society 6
Austin, Thomas 16
Australian Quarantine and Inspection Service (AQIS) 10

B
Barkly, Sir Henry 6
biological control (of pests) 11, 17

C
cane toad 2, 3, 5, 14, 15
carp 3, 18, 19
cat 3, 8, 9, 12, 13
Cook, Captain James 24

D
domestic animals 4
donkey 3, 26
drought 23

E
ecosystem 5, 28, 30
extinction 8, 12, 16, 28

F
feral animals 3, 4, 5, 6, 8, 26, 30
First Fleet 7, 13, 22, 27

G
goat 3, 27
Gordonvale, Queensland 14

H
Horse 3, 22, 23

I
immunocontraception 31
indigenous people 25

M
Murray-Darling River Basin 18
Murray River 18, 19
myxomatosis 17, 30, 31

N
Northern Territory 14, 22, 24, 25

P
Paterson, 'Banjo' 22
pig 3, 24
Prospect Reservoir, Sydney 18

R
rabbit 3, 16, 17
rabbit calicivirus disease (RCD) 17
rabies 12
red fox 3, 20

T
Townshead Island, Queensland 11
Toxoplasmosis 12

W
water buffalo 3, 25